AMBITIOUS ABBEY BAKES

Written by
Abbey Duplaga

Illustrated by
O.J. Diomedi & Andrew Thomas

DEDICATION

This book is dedicated to my mom, aunts, sisters, nieces, nephews, and cousins. Thank you for the memories in the kitchen and making baking such a fun and passionate activity throughout the years. I have learned much and have made some of the best memories. Love you all!

Copyright © 2023 by Abbey Duplaga.
All rights reserved.
Printed in the United States of America.
ISBN: 979-8-218-29250-8

TABLE OF CONTENTS

Letter to Baker..4
Before You Get Started..5
Equipment..6
Recipes..9
Baking Words..26
Notes...28
Pictures..30

LETTER TO BAKER

Hello, fellow baker!
    I have a passion and a love for baking and I'm excited to share some of my favorite recipes with you. Throughout the pages of this book, you will find fifteen different recipes as well as pictures of myself and family members baking.

Baking is something I grew up enjoying. My mother and aunt are great bakers and I enjoyed watching them and learning from them in the kitchen or in their bakery, Cookiepops, just like in my story, "Ambitious Abbey".

All of the recipes in this book are intended to be baked with an adult helper. From a young girl and to this day, I have enjoyed baking and creating in the kitchen, which is why I wanted to create this book and share one of my passions with you. It's my hope that you grow to love the recipes and enjoy making them. Most importantly, I hope you enjoy quality time in the kitchen with loved ones as you create memories and sweet treats to share!

Love,
Abbey

BEFORE YOU GET STARTED

Before you get started, there are a few important rules to remember in the kitchen.

1 - Read the recipe and make sure you have all of the ingredients and equipment you need.

2 - Wash your hands and protect your clothes by putting on an apron. If you have long hair, tie it back to keep it out of the way.

3 - Always have an adult help with the oven.

4 - When measuring liquids, be sure measuring cup is on a flat surface. When measuring dry. be sure the ingredients are even.

EQUIPMENT

Pictured below are basic items you will need to use during baking any of the recipes throughout this baking book. Each item has a number on it that ties to the key listed.

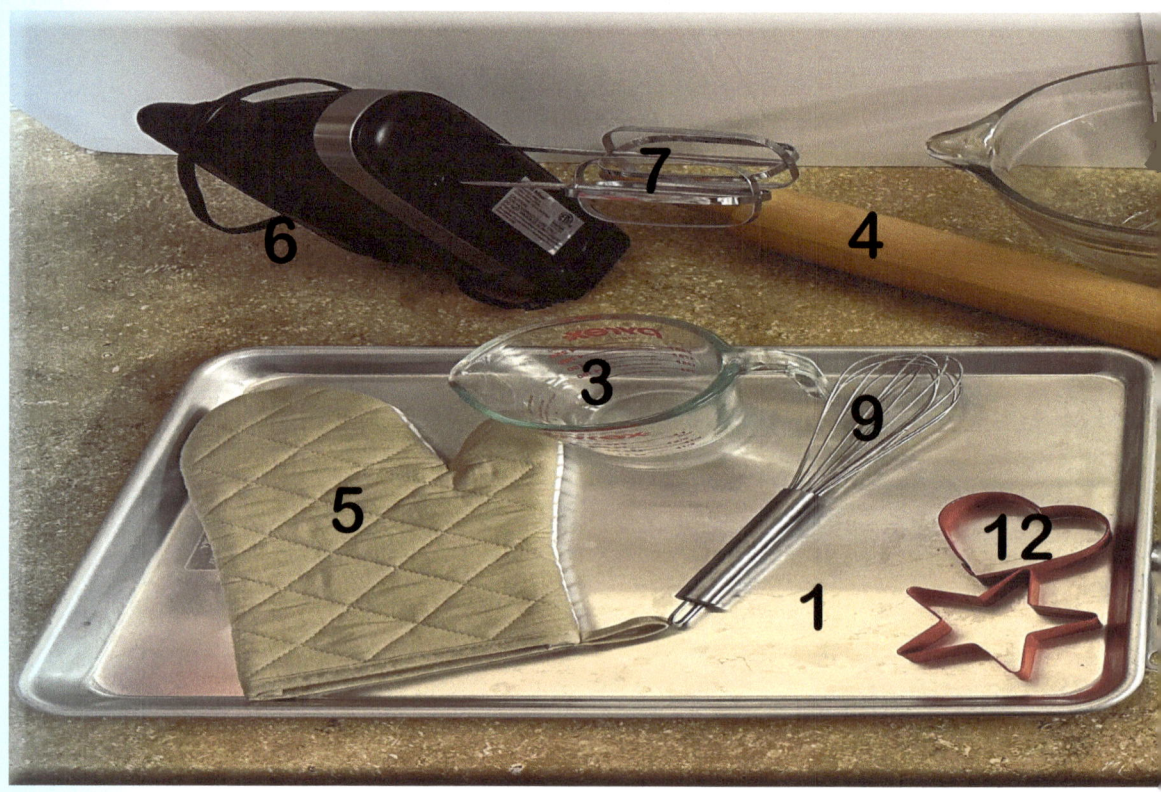

1 - Cookie Sheet
2 - Mixing Bowl
3 - Measuring Cup
4 - Rolling Pin
5 - Oven Mitt
6 - Mixer
7 - Beaters
9 - Whisk
10 - Measuring Spoons
11 - Spatula
12 - Cookie Cutter
13 - Parchment Paper
14 - Piping Bag
15 - 9" x 13" Baking Pan

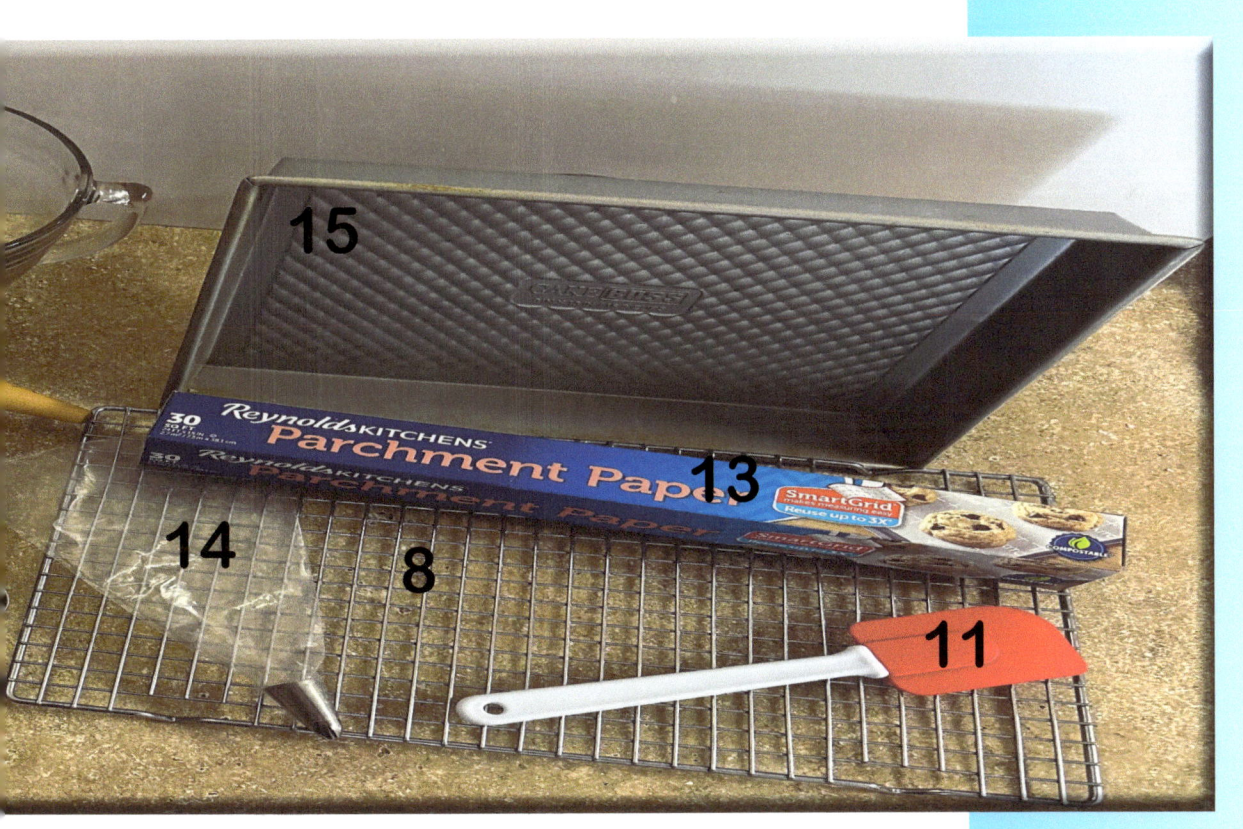

* Most recipes are original recipes from my Grandma Jeanie's kitchen!

RECIPES

Abbey's Favorite Cookie..10
Sugar Cookie Cut-outs...11
Perfect Oatmeal Cookies 12
Peanut Butter Oatmeal Balls..13
No-Bake Cookies...14
Crunchy Cornflake Hearts..15
Crispy Stars..16
Braided Hearts..17
M&M Cookies..18
Peanut Butter Cookies..19
Snickerdoodles...20
Cake Pops..21
Chocolate Crinkles..22
Pancakes..23
Chocolate Chip Cookies...24

ABBEY'S FAVORITE COOKIE

Makes 20 Cookies

INGREDIENTS:

1 box yellow cake mix
1/3 cup canola oil
2 eggs
1 cup confectioners' sugar
1 cup red candy melts (melted)

DIRECTIONS:

1 - Mix together cake mix, canola oil and eggs. Batter will be thick.
2 - Shape dough into 1-inch balls or use a 1-inch cookie scoop.
Roll dough into confectioners' sugar.
* If you find your dough is too soft to roll, you can refrigerate for 30 minutes before rolling.
3 - Bake at 350 degrees on parchment paper lined cookie sheet for 8-10 minutes or until cookies begin to crack just slightly.
4 — Draw on hearts with your melted candy melts (following the directions on the package to melt) by using the non-bristle end of an artist paint brush or a piping bag.

SUGAR COOKIE CUT-OUTS

Makes 30-60 Cookies

INGREDIENTS:

Cookie Dough:
1 ½ sticks margarine
1 cup sugar
2 eggs
1 teaspoon vanilla
1 teaspoon baking powder
½ teaspoon salt
3 cups flour

Icing:
2 cups powdered sugar
1 teaspoon vanilla
1/4 cup milk

DIRECTIONS:

1 – Cream together margarine and sugar.
2 – Beat in eggs and vanilla.
3 – Add baking powder, salt, and flour.
4 – Roll out dough with rolling pin until flat and even (1/4 in thick). Cut with cookie cutters dipped in flour to reduce sticking.
5 – Bake at 350 degrees on parchment paper lined cookie sheet for 7-10 minutes.

*If you would like to make icing glaze to decorate with once the cookies are cooled:
Mix powdered sugar, vanilla, and milk until smooth. You can divide this mixture up and add food coloring to create different colored glazes. Decorate the cookies and sprinkle with colored sugars.

PERFECT OATMEAL COOKIES

Makes 16 Cookies

INGREDIENTS:

½ cup butter, softened
½ cup white sugar
½ cup brown sugar
1 egg
½ teaspoon vanilla
1 cup flour
½ teaspoon baking soda
½ teaspoon salt
¾ teaspoon cinnamon
½ cups old fashioned oats
Raisins and chopped walnuts (handful of each)

DIRECTIONS:

1 - Cream together butter, white sugar, brown sugar. Beat in egg, then vanilla. In separate bowl, mix together flour, baking soda, salt, and cinnamon. Add this mixture to the creamed mixture. Fold in raisins and walnuts. Fold in oats.
2 - Cover and refrigerate dough for one hour.
3 - Roll dough into balls and place on two parchment paper lined cookie sheets (8 cookies per sheet).
Dip a wet fork into white sugar and use it to slightly press down on each ball before baking.
4 - Bake at 375 for 8-10 minutes.

PEANUT BUTTER OATMEAL BALLS

Makes 14 Balls

INGREDIENTS:

1 cup old fashioned oats
½ cup peanut butter
1/3 cup honey
1 teaspoon vanilla

DIRECTIONS:

1 - Mix together oats, peanut butter, honey, and vanilla.
2 - Shape dough into 1 ½ -inch or bite sized balls.
3 – Place on parchment paper to set.

NO-BAKE COOKIES

Makes 30 Cookies

INGREDIENTS:

2 cups sugar
¼ cup cocoa
½ cup milk
4 tablespoons margarine
½ cup peanut butter
1 teaspoon vanilla
2 cups quick oats

DIRECTIONS:

1 – Combine and boil for one minute the sugar, cocoa, milk, and margarine. Remove from heat.
2 – Once removed from heat, add, peanut butter, salt, vanilla, and oats.
3 – Mix well and drop by teaspoon onto wax paper to dry and set.
4 – Once dried and set, peel from wax paper and enjoy!

CRUNCHY CORNFLAKE HEARTS

Makes 10-12 Hearts

INGREDIENTS:

½ cup butter
6 cups mini marshmallows
6 cups cornflake cereal
1 teaspoon food coloring of choice

DIRECTIONS:

1 – Place cornflakes into a large bowl and set aside.
2 – Melt butter in a saucepan on medium heat. Add marshmallows and stir until melted. Stir in food coloring.
3 – Add marshmallow mixture to the cornflakes and stir until cornflakes are completely covered.
4 – Lay out parchment paper on counter, and drop large spoonfuls of cornflakes onto the paper. Lightly butter or grease hands and use your fingers to shape them into hearts.
5 – Let set and dry before removal from paper.

CRISPY STARS

Makes 8 Stars

INGREDIENTS:

3 tablespoons butter
1 10 ounce bag marshmallows
6 cups crispy rice cereal

DIRECTIONS:

1 – Melt butter and marshmallows in pan and cook until smooth.
2 – Add crispy rice cereal until completely mixed and coated.
3 – Using a spatula dipped in hot water, spread mixture into a 9 x 13 inch baking dish.
4 – Let cool.
5 – Once cooled, use a star-shaped cookie cutter to cut as many stars as possible.
Sprinkle stars with nonpareils or sprinkles of choice.

BRAIDED HEARTS

Makes 14 Hearts

INGREDIENTS:

½ cup Crisco
½ cup margarine
cup confectioners' sugar
egg
½ teaspoon almond extract
teaspoon vanilla
teaspoon salt
½ cups flour
ed food coloring

DIRECTIONS:

1 — Cream together Crisco, margarine, confectioners' sugar, egg, almond extract, and vanilla.
2 — Add salt and flour.
3 — Divide dough in half. Add red food coloring to ½ of the batter and leaving the other half plain.
4 — Roll a 9 inch strip out of each color. Add flour if still too wet. Also use flour on hand and fingers to roll the strips if needed. Lay them parallel to one another (side by side) and press slightly together and transfer to cookie sheet. Twist and shape into a heart. Sprinkle with sugar.
5 — Place on cookie sheets lined with parchment paper and bake at 350 degrees for 13 minutes.
*Note: This is the most difficult cookie to make of all recipes in the book due to the nature of the difficulty of rolling anf twisting dough into hearts.

M&M COOKIES

Makes 30 Cookies

INGREDIENTS:

1 cup unsalted butter (softened)
1 cup brown sugar
½ cup white sugar
2 teaspoons vanilla
2 eggs
1 teaspoon baking soda
1 teaspoon salt
2 ½ cups flour
1 ½ cups M&M's

DIRECTIONS:

1 – Cream together butter, brown sugar, white sugar.
2 – Add vanilla and eggs.
3 – Add baking soda, salt, and flour.
4 – Stir in 1 cup of M&M's, saving the other ½ cup to decorate tops of cookies before baking in oven.
5 – Roll into 1 inch balls and place on parchment paper lined cookie sheets.
6 – Add a few M&Ms to the tops of each.
7 – Bake at 350 degrees for approximately 10 minutes.

PEANUT BUTTER COOKIES

Makes 48 Cookies

INGREDIENTS:

1 cup butter
1 cup sugar
1 cup brown sugar
1 teaspoon vanilla
2 eggs
1 cup peanut butter
3 teaspoons baking soda
3 cups flour
Dash of salt

DIRECTIONS:

1 – Cream together butter, sugar, brown sugar, and vanilla.
2 – Add eggs and beat.
3 – Stir in peanut butter.
4 – Add salt, baking soda, and flour.
5 – Form into 1 ½ inch balls and place on cookie sheet lined with parchment paper. Flatten with fork. Use flour on fork if too sticky.
6 – Bake at 375 degrees for 10 minutes.

SNICKERDOODLES

Makes 30 Cookies

INGREDIENTS:

1 cup butter
1 ½ cups sugar
2 eggs
2 teaspoons cream of tartar
1 teaspoon baking soda
2 ¾ cups flour

DIRECTIONS:

1 – Cream butter, sugar, eggs, cream of tartar, baking soda, flour, and salt.
2 – Chill dough mixture for 30 minutes.
3 – Roll into 1-inch balls and then roll the balls into a bowl of a mixture of cinnamon and sugar. Place on parchment paper lined cookie sheet. Press down slightly on each ball with the palm of your hand.
4 – Bake at 325 degrees for 8 minutes.

CAKE POPS

Makes 32 Pops

INGREDIENTS:

1 box chocolate cake mix
1 can chocolate icing
Red vanilla chocolate candy wafers
1 bag of sticks
½ teaspoon salt

DIRECTIONS:

1 – Bake cake according to directions on back of box in a 9x13 inch pan.
2 – Let cake cool on a baking rack.
3 – Once cool, remove from pan and crumble cake into fine pieces in a mixing bowl.
4 – Add ½ of the container of icing to the bowl and work with hands until it makes a dense batter.
5 – Roll into one inch balls and place them on a parchment paper lined tray. Place in the refrigerator for 30 minutes.
6 – Place red wafers in a bowl in microwave on 1-minute intervals and mix until completely melted.
*Add 1 Teaspoon of spry (Crisco) if chocolate is too thick to give a thinner consistency. Add more as needed.
7 – Dip the end of a stick into the melted chocolate and insert into a ball. Pick the ball up by the stick and completely submerge it into the chocolate until covered. Tap off excess and apply sprinkles while wet.
8 – Place on wax paper lined cookie sheet. Let dry.

CHOCOLATE CRINKLES

Makes 36 Cookies

INGREDIENTS:

2 cups white sugar
1 cup unsweetened cocoa powder
½ cup canola oil
4 large eggs
2 teaspoons vanilla extract
2 cups all-purpose flour
2 teaspoons baking powder
½ teaspoon salt

DIRECTIONS:

1 – Mix white sugar, unsweetened cocoa powder and canola oil together in a medium bowl. Beat in eggs, one at a time, until combined. Stir in vanilla with spatula.

2 – Combine flour, baking powder, and salt in another mixing bowl. Stir together. Gradually beat dry ingredients into wet ingredients until thoroughly mixed.

3 – Cover dough and place in refrigerator for at least four hours.

4 – Preheat oven to 350 degrees. Line cookie sheets with parchment paper.

5 – Roll or scoop chilled dough into 1 ½ inch balls. Roll each ball in confectioners' sugar until fully coated and covered. Place on cookie sheet.

6 – Bake for 10-12 minutes. Let cool on the cookie sheet for 2 minutes then transfer to a flat surface or cooling rack with a spatula.

PANCAKES

Makes 7 Hearts

INGREDIENTS:

1 large egg
1 1/2 cups all-purpose flour
1 tablespoon baking powder.
1/2 teaspoon salt
1 1/4 cup milk
2 tablespoons sugar
4 tablespoons butter (melted)

DIRECTIONS:

1 – Mix together all ingredients in mixing bowl using a whisk to make smooth consistency, but do not over mix once smooth consistency is accomplished.
2 – Preheat skillet to medium heat. After warm and reaching temperature, spray skillet with nonstick cooking spray.
3 – Center cookie cutter in skillet and pour in batter about 1/3 of the way up the cookie cutter.
*You can also make silver dollar pancakes or larger sized pancakes without using a cookie cutter. Shape and size are according to preference.
4 – When bubbles are visible, flip over, remove cookie cutter, and let cook on the other side until a golden brown.
5 – Add syrup and enjoy!

CHOCOLATE CHIP COOKIES

Makes 48 Cookies

INGREDIENTS:

2 1/4 cups all-purpose flour
1 teaspoon baking soda
1 teaspoon salt
1 cup (2 sticks) butter, softened
3/4 cup granulated sugar
3/4 cup packed brown sugar
1 teaspoon vanilla extract
2 large eggs
1 (11.5 ounce) bag of semi-sweet or milk chocolate chips

INSTRUCTIONS:

1 – Combine and mix together flour, baking soda, and salt in a small bowl.
2 – Cream together butter, sugar, brown sugar, and vanilla extract in large bowl until creamy. Add eggs, one at a time - beating well after each addition.
3 – Add flour slowly and gradually until well mixed.
4 – Finally, fold in chocolate chips.
5 – Drop into teaspoon sized drops on cookie sheet lined with parchment paper.
6 – Bake at 375 degrees for 9 minutes.

BAKING WORDS

Below is a list of baking words and simple explanations used in the different recipes in this book.

Bake – Cook a food in the oven.
Beat – Quickly and thoroughly mix ingredients together.
Boil – Heat a liquid over high heat until it bubbles.
Chill – Cool food in the refrigerator.
Chop – Cut into smaller pieces.
Cool – Let food sit at room temperature until it's no longer warm to touch
Cream – Beat ingredients together with a mixer until light and fluffy.
Fold – Mix one ingredient into another gently and gradually.
Grease – Lightly coat baking sheet with oil or butter to prevent sticking.
Melt – Using heat to turn a solid into a liquid.
Roll out – Flatten dough into a smooth and even layer using a rolling pin.
Stir – Mix ingredients together to combine.
Whisk – Quickly stir ingredients using a whisk or a fork.

BAKING NOTES

BAKING NOTES

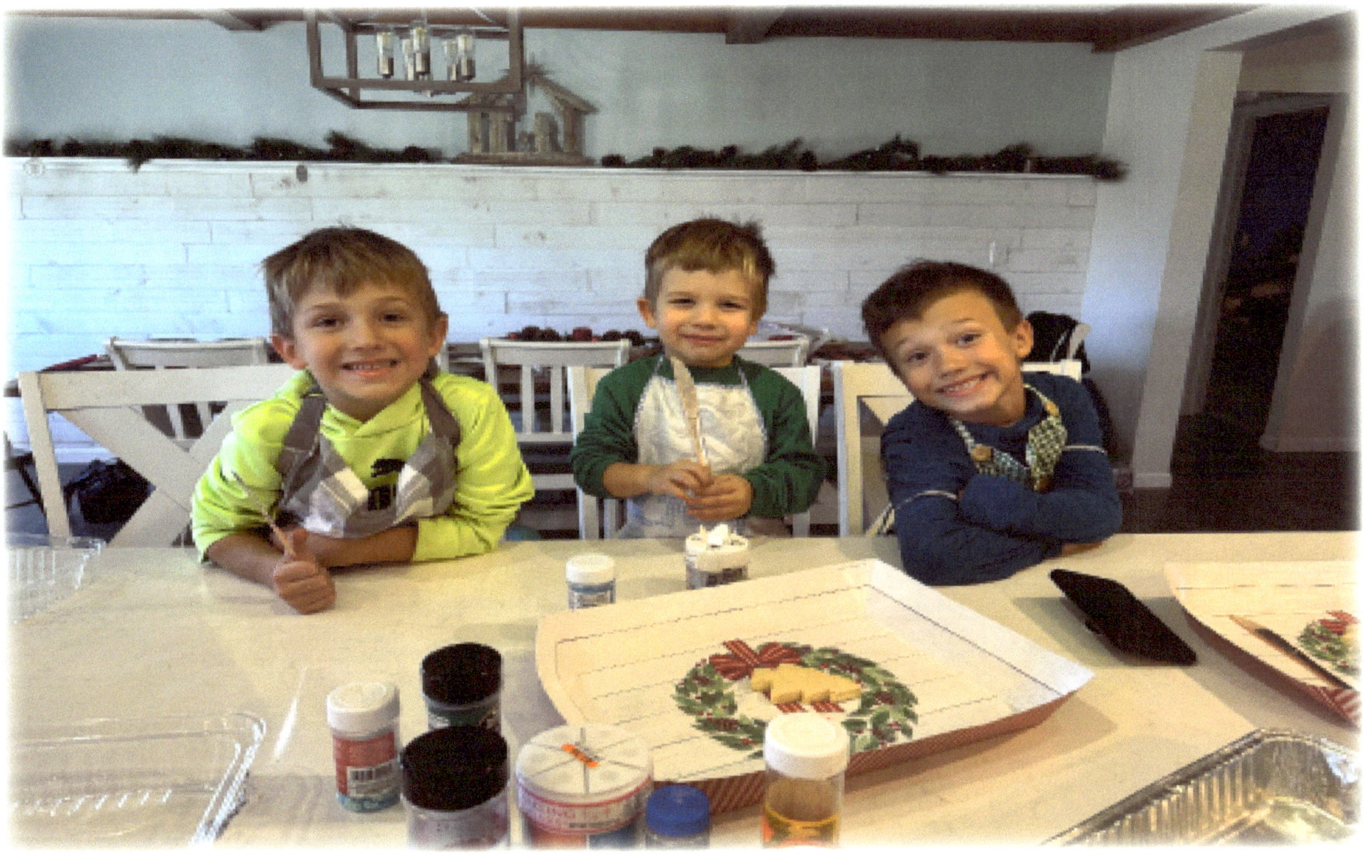

Official
COOKIE

Official
COOKIE
Official
COOKIE

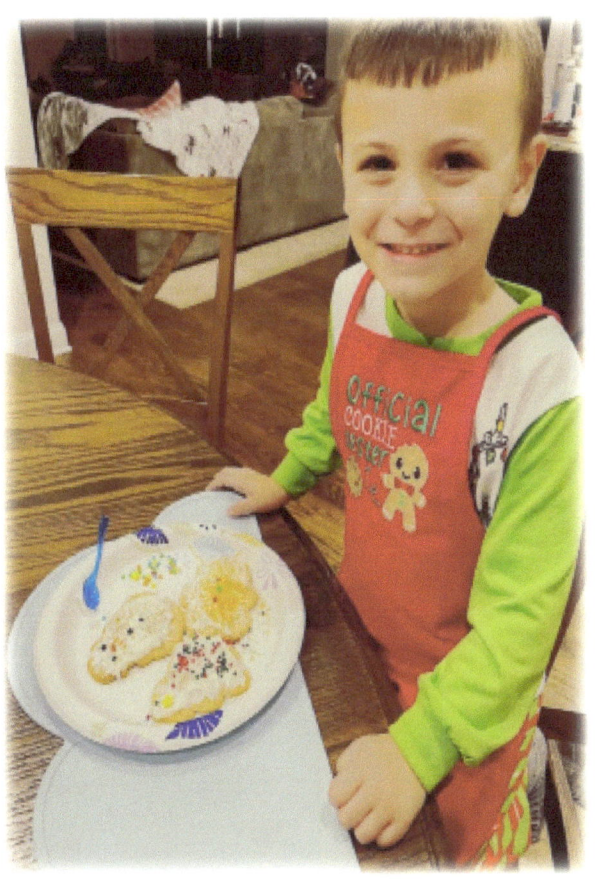

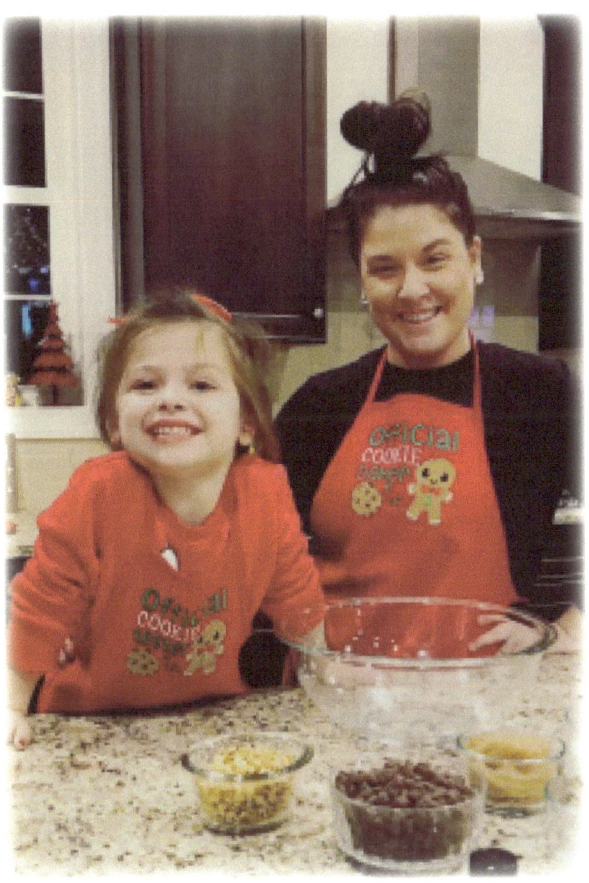

www.ingramcontent.com/pod-product-compliance
Lightning Source LLC
Chambersburg PA
CBHW041412010526
44107CB00015B/1142